Six Sugars in My Coffee:

The Sweet Words of Middle School Poets

Coconut Avenue, Inc. - Suggested Retail Prices

Six Sugars in My Coffee: The Sweet Words of Middle School Poets
The 2013-2014 Middle School Students of St. Joseph Catholic Academy
Kenosha, Wisconsin

Release Date:	October 31 , 2014
Trade Paper ISBN:	978-0-9837499-4-3
Trade Paper List Price:	$12.95 US
E-Book ISBN (PDF):	978-0-9837499-5-0
E-Book List Price:	$9.95 US
Kindle ISBN:	978-0-9837499-6-7
Kindle List Price:	$9.99 US

Publisher's prices higher in other countries.
Prices subject to change without notice.
For current pricing information, please visit
Coconut Avenue, Inc. online: coconutavenue.com

PRAISE FOR

Six Sugars in My Coffee:
The Sweet Words of Middle School Poets

"This book is full of clever insights and humor from the minds of middle school poets. I literally laughed out loud many times as I read these poems. This book will leave footprints in your heart!"

> **Polly A. Bauer**, co-author of the award winning book *The Plastic Effect: How Urban Legends Influence the Use and Misuse of Credit Cards.*

"These poetic musings illustrate the creativity, thoughtfulness, and humor of our next generation of leaders. How exciting it is to peek into the minds of middle school poets!"

> **Amanda Cole**, President, GadgitKids

"Creative and humorous, this book brings to life the poetic words of middle school students with awe, wonder, and delight!"

> **Charity Beck**, Founder and CEO of *Positive Impact Magazine*

―――――

Other titles by St. Joseph Catholic Academy:

Exceptional: The Inspired Words of Middle School Poets

Six Sugars in My Coffee:

The Sweet Words of Middle School Poets

Sixth Grade Middle School Class
2013-2014

St. Joseph Catholic Academy
Kenosha, Wisconsin

kenoshastjoseph.com

Coconut Avenue®
Chicago, Illinois USA

The Creative Avenue for Best Selling Authors®

Copyright © 2014 by St. Joseph Catholic Academy, Kenosha, Wisconsin
All rights reserved.
Published in the United States by:
Coconut Avenue, Inc. - coconutavenue.com
Edited by: Leslie D. Edwards
School Editor: Matthew Giunti
Cover and Interior Design: Nicole Eckenrode
Cover Photograph: Copyright © by Veer, Inc.
Used under license from Veer, Inc.

No part of this book may be produced by any mechanical, photographic, or electronic process, or in the form of a phonographic or video recording; and it may not be used in any retrieval system, currently known or yet to be developed, transmitted, or otherwise copied for public or private use, other than under the "fair use" provisions of copyright law as brief quotations embodied in articles and reviews, without prior written permission of the publisher.

Trade paper ISBN: 978-0-9837499-4-3.

Suggested retail price: $12.95 USD.

1st Edition, October 31, 2014 - Printed in the United States of America.

Coconut Avenue®, *The Creative Avenue For Best Selling Authors*®, and the *Coconut Avenue graphic*® are all registered U.S. Trademarks of Coconut Avenue, Inc. *Six Sugars In My Coffee: The Sweet Words of Middle School Poets*™ is a trademark of Coconut Avenue, Inc. The other trademarks used herein are the property of their respective owners. Unauthorized use of any of these trademarks is prohibited. Book cover design and internal design layout Copyright © 2014 by Coconut Avenue, Inc. All rights reserved.

TABLE OF CONTENTS

Foreword *11*
Sixth Grade Poets 2013-2014 .... *13*
Poems *15*

   I'm No Poet *by St. Joseph's Grade 6* **16**

   Friends *by Elizabeth Alia* **18**

   My Dream *by Elizabeth Alia* **19**

   Flowers *by Sophia Barrington-Nate* **20**

   I Can Write a Poem *by Sophia Barrington-Nate* **21**

   Baseball *by Austin Bencs* **22**

   St. Germain *by Austin Bencs* **23**

   Pie *by Ellie Bernhardt* **24**

   Soccer *by Ellie Bernhardt* **25**

   S'mores *by Megan Berry* **26**

   Spring Break *by Megan Berry* **27**

   Lego Ships *by Brendan Bjork* **28**

   Summer *by Brendan Bjork* **29**

   Best Friends *by Mary Bolog* **30**

   Four Haikus *by Mary Bolog* **31**

   Fear *by Grace Borchardt* **32**

   Three Haikus *by Grace Borchardt* **33**

   Ice Skating *by Arianna Bosco* **34**

   Starbucks Trip *by Arianna Bosco* **36**

   Wolf *by James Castro* **37**

Angels *by James Castro*	38
Friendship *by Kara Clark*	39
Four Haikus *by Kara Clark*	40
Day with Dad *by Trey Connolly*	41
Poem *by Trey Connolly*	42
Sherlock Holmes *by Claudia Copher*	43
The Ood *by Claudia Copher*	44
Ice Cream *by Elizabeth Curry*	45
Say "Cheese!" *by Elizabeth Curry*	46
Frogs *by Katie Dabrowski*	47
Wolves *by Katie Dabrowski*	48
Piano *by Alexandra Daher*	49
Pineapples *by Alexandra Daher*	50
The Chicago Cubs *by Matthew Deacon*	51
Summer *by Matthew Deacon*	52
Bears *by Emily Diab*	53
Willy Wonka *by Emily Diab*	54
Woodman's *by Tim Evans*	55
Tiger *by Tim Evans*	56
Friendship *by Jalen Fayne*	57
I Love to Eat *by Jalen Fayne*	58
Music *by Reyna Ferraro*	59
Shopping *by Reyna Ferraro*	60
Nature *by Ben Franklin*	61
Crush *by Ben Franklin*	62

Searching for My Dreams   *by Katherine Gapinski* 63

A Friend   *by Katherine Gapinski*..64

Eagles   *by Jake Gessert* 65

Squirrels   *by Jake Gessert* 66

Nature   *by Jena Gessert* 67

Summer Activity   *by Jena Gessert* 68

Baseball Night   *by Dominik Gillespie* 69

Sports   *by Dominik Gillespie* 70

Cupcake   *by Lara Gonzalez* 71

The Flower   *by Lara Gonzalez* 72

Soccer   *by Katie Hamm* 73

Three Haikus   *by Katie Hamm* 74

Sweets!   *by Stella Harrington* 75

The Bearded Man   *by Stella Harrington* 76

The Seasons   *by Eliana Hudock*..77

Animals   *by Eliana Hudock* 78

Bird   *by Valentin Iaquinta* 79

Flight   *by Valentin Iaquinta* 80

The Wonderful Day   *by Emma Iwen* 81

Baby Animals   *by Emma Iwen* 82

Cookies   *by Emma Johnson* 83

Positive   *by Emma Johnson* 84

Cereal: A Poem in Seven Haikus   *by Keely Kennedy* 85

Hunting   *by Keely Kennedy* 86

Country Life   *by Matthew Knapp*...88

Hunting *by Matthew Knapp*	90
My Mother *by Josephine Knight*	91
Monsters *by Josephine Knight*	92
Five Seconds of Summer *by Katie Kormylo*	93
Fruit *by Katie Kormylo*	94
Sorry, Gotta Run! *by Katherine Lesavich*	95
Love *by Katherine Lesavich*	96
My Dog *by Matthew Lesperance*	97
Young Love *by Leah Madden*	98
Two Haikus *by Leah Madden*	99
Hamburgers *by Anthony Madrigrano*	100
Lobster *by Anthony Madrigrano*	101
Rosie *by Solei Maj*	102
Seasons *by Solei Maj*	103
Soccer *by Ellie Mandli*	104
Lemonade *by Ellie Mandli*	105
The Tippity-Tap-Tap Bubble Wrap *Mia Marotti*	106
I Hate Pumpkin Pie *Mia Marotti*	107
Push *by Claire Mayew Sherman*	108
Life *by Claire Mayew Sherman*	109
Flowers *by Abygale McGonigle*	110
Pigs *by Abygale McGonigle*	111
Mothers *by Marlena Moore*	112
Spring Awakening *by Marlena Moore*	113
Family Trip *by Natalie Murphy*	114

The Mist *by Michael Pienkos*	115
A Bad Morning *by Michael Pienkos*	116
Books *by Bernadette Pitt-Payne*	117
Roller Coasters *by Bernadette Pitt-Payne*	118
Friends *by Brendon Rafferty*	119
Perseverance *by Brendon Rafferty*	120
MLB *by Jake Reigel*	121
Summer *by Jake Reigel*	122
Pizza *by Tess Roberts*	123
Sports *by Tess Roberts*	124
Music *by Seth Rosen*	125
Two Friends *by Seth Rosen*	126
My Mother *by Jonathan Rudd*	127
Poor Old Jake *by Jonathan Rudd*	128
Haikus About My Life *by Caleb Ryherd*	129
Museum *by Caleb Ryherd*	130
Worms *by Mia Scarlato*	131
Bella: Two Haikus *by Mia Scarlato*	132
Cookies *by Gabriella Schneider*	133
Lola *by Gabriella Schneider*	134
Car Ride *by Emily Schwerdtfeger*	135
Three Haikus *by Emily Schwerdtfeger*	136
Spring *by Matthew Spadafore*	137
The Stanley Cup *by Matthew Spadafore*	138
Love *by Ryan Spadafore*	139

Four Haikus *by Ryan Spadafore* 140

In Summer *by Joseph Stapleton* 141

Rainy Day *by Joseph Stapleton* 142

Dogs *by Ben VerHagen* 143

Pasta *by Ben VerHagen* 144

Copyright/Trademark Disclaimer 147

St. Joseph Catholic Academy 148

About Coconut Avenue®, Inc. 151

Coconut Avenue®, Inc., Award Winning Book 152

Coconut Avenue®, Inc., Award Winning Publishing Company .. 153

Other Coconut Avenue® Products 155

Foreword

I've taught at every grade level between first and eighth grade in my career, and I often think that the height of student creativity occurs in sixth grade. Prior to that, students are still amassing their knowledge of literature's rules and conventions, often resulting in work that, while undoubtedly imaginative, can lack structure and coherence. As they make their way into the higher grades, pop culture, social media, and peer expectations seem to have a constricting effect on young imaginations. Now, instead of a wide-open creative landscape, students begin to follow the beaten paths of Disney, video games, teen novels, and superhero movies. By the time they reach high school, the footprints of mass culture can be seen all over this once untouched creative environment. Suddenly, creative writing becomes about "doing it the right way."

It's this crossroad between pure childish imagination and the initial understanding of literary structure and convention that makes teaching sixth grade so delightful for me. While some days come easier than others (on both sides), I'm still amazed by the level of curiosity and enthusiasm that they can bring to a creative writing assignment. As they take their places in a world that seems to value creativity, originality, and inspiration less and less all the time, I pray they never lose that joy in inventive mind-play.

For this assignment, students were asked to compile a poetry portfolio consisting of one rhymed poem, one free verse poem, and a third poem-type of their own choosing (out of which two apiece were chosen). So, in this collection, you will encounter formal poems and unstructured poems. And haikus. Boy, do sixth graders love haikus! I hope you enjoy them as much as we enjoyed creating and sharing them.

Matthew Guinti
Middle School Language and Writing Teacher

St. Joseph Catholic Academy
Kenosha, Wisconsin
May 2014

Sixth Grade Poets 2013-2014

St. Joseph Catholic Academy
Kenosha, Wisconsin

Copyright © 2014, St. Joseph Catholic Academy. All Rights Reserved.

Poems

I'm No Poet

by St. Joseph's Grade 6

I'm no poet because I don't have the skills.
I'm no poet because I'd rather write stories and draw.
I'm no poet because I don't know what poetry is.
I'm no poet because I don't like poetry.
I'm no poet because I would rather play piano.
I'm no poet because I'd rather play soccer.
I'm no poet because I like reading waaaay more than writing.
I'm no poet because I don't inspire people.
I'm no poet because I'm bad at following multi-step directions and concentrating on just one thing.
I'm no poet because poetry is not my cup of tea, I plea.
I'm no poet because I'd rather play video games.
I'm no poet because I'd rather be a dancer.
I'm no poet because I've gotta run.
I'm no poet because I don't like poems.
I'm no poet because I'd rather read essays.
I'm no poet because I've never been interested in anything!
I'm no poet because I'm a unicorn in disguise.
I'm no poet because I'm just a kid.
I'm no poet because it's too much work.
I'm no poet because I can't spell, or write well, and certainly by now you can tell!
I'm no poet because I'm a shark and I'm really hungry right now.
I'm no poet because I don't like to rhyme and it takes too much time.
I'm no poet because I'm not good at choosing exciting topics.
I'm no poet because I don't always get the assignment.
I'm no poet because I'd rather be drawing.

I'm no poet because I don't like poetry at all.
I'm no poet because I'd rather be hunting.
I'm no poet because I'm not a good writer.
I'm no poet because I'd rather be at home sleeping.
I'm no poet because writing isn't my thing; I spend most of
	my time sitting in a dark boat, on the depths of the
	ocean, plotting my next scheme.
I'm no poet because I'd rather be eating.
I'm no poet because I have better things to do like torture my
	sister.
I'm no poet because I'd rather be shopping.
I'm no poet because I'm stuck in an alternate universe.
I'm no poet because my pencil is broken.
I'm no poet because I'm lazy.
I'm no poet because poetry is plain and boring.
I'm no poet because I've not yet found any inspiration.
I'm no poet because I'm too fabulous to be a poet.
I'm no poet because I'm too cool for school.
I'm no poet because I'm a teddy bear.
I'm no poet because my fingers were bitten off by a dragon.
I'm no poet because I don't really like poetry.
I'm no poet because I'm not really familiar with all the
	different types of poems.
I'm no poet because there are always people who criticize my
	work.
I'm no poet because poetry creeps me out.
I'm no poet because I don't practice writing poems.
I'm no poet because I don't want to be one.
I'm no poet because I have better things to do.
I'm no poet because I hate writing!

Hey, wait! I just wrote a poem!
I guess I am a poet!

Friends

by Elizabeth Alia

Kara is a redhead
And she really loves her bed.
Stella is a big mouth
Like a jumbo megaphone.

Arianna has long lashes
And dashes on the ice.
While Kelsey's out in nature
Trying to catch mice.

Caroline's really pretty
And super-duper smart.
Then there's tiny little Chloe
A phenomenal star.

Katie's very funny
With flawless ice blue eyes.
And Solei is my awesome neighbor
With an extremely awesome dog.

Alyssa is like my sister
Who is often very happy.
And Sydney is my blonde buddy
Who laughs at random things.

All my friends are special
Although there's too many to name
But these are my best buddies
Who will always remain the same.

My Dream

by Elizabeth Alia

This morning I fell down the stairs
And ran into some chairs.
My brother hit me with a bat
Then I fell on my cat.
I had a real bad headache
And my mom was at the lake,
So I waddled to my sister's room
And she smacked me with a broom.
So I took a hard fall onto the floor
And bumped my head on the door.
I thought I was about to die
But then I started to cry
And I wanted to scream
But then I realized it was just a dream.

Flowers

by Sophia Barrington-Nate

Flowers have power.
Color power.
They are yellow, red, pink, blue, green, and more.
They make a woman happy to see all the colors.
They can fill a person with joy
When they see a bundle of flowers.
Flowers, flowers,
Yellow, pink, blue,
Green, red, white,
Orange, orange-red, greenish-blue.
Flowers.

I Can Write a Poem

by Sophia Barrington-Nate

I can write a poem because…
I can write a poem because poems are cool.
I can write a poem because I am not playing with my brother.
I can write a poem because I have no homework.
I can write a poem because I am not playing on the Wii.
I can write a poem because I'm not playing games with my family.
I can write a poem because they are fun to write.
I can write a poem because I'm not shopping with my mom.
I can write a poem because I'm not going to my brother's hockey game.
I can write a poem because it is quiet in the house.
I can write a poem because I'm not coloring.
I can write a poem because I learned how to write them.
I can write a poem.

Baseball

by Austin Bencs

My dad tells me to get clothes on,
He gets me a Gatorade to drink.
I think of how I'm going to play,
I warm up a little bit.
The game starts, the crowd gets rowdy.
We are guests, so, on the field first.
Three up, three down!
We are up to hit,
We get three runs!
Inning is over 3-0.
They hit and get four runs.
Coach gives a talk,
We are pumped up!
We get four more runs and we are excited!
We win the game!
I fall asleep knowing the night was good.

St. Germain

by Austin Bencs

The long six-hour drive,
The smell of the woods,
The feeling of sand on your feet.
I love the restaurants that are only in St. Germain,
I love not winning bingo,
I love jumping off the raft,
I love going to a pub & grill.
I play skill crane
And darts.
I love the cook-outs,
The people are nice.
We prank my Aunt,
We laugh for a long time!
We enjoy the night.
We play card games
And sit around a fire,
Talk about times before.
Enjoy thousands of different sodas,
Enjoy the best ice cream in Eagle River!

Pie

by Ellie Bernhardt

The strong scent of cinnamon
Tickles my nose,
As I assist my mom
As she bakes her well-known
Apple pie.
The apples I am cutting
Make a good smell
As the sharp, shiny knife carves
Into their bright white flesh.
The squishy dough forms in my hands,
As I knead it back and forth
And back and forth.
My whole family looks forward to eating it.
Always helping themselves to seconds
Or even thirds.
I imagine scooping little pieces of it into my mouth
And how warm and soft it is.
It is the perfect golden brown shade.
My mom's apple pie reminds me of great memories.

Soccer

by Ellie Bernhardt

I sprint as I cry in pain,
Coach yells, "RUN, PASS, SCORE!"

Blocking out all the screaming
And the crazy noises from the sidelines,
I dash through five tough defenders
With everything that I've got.

Out of breath, I use the last of my energy I can use
To score the winning goal.

The ball zigzags through my bright green cleats
As I fly through many people that
Get in my way.

Five seconds left in the game.
Will it make it in?
My fingers are crossed.

All the pressure is on the ball and me,
As it flies over the field where I am
And flies too high for the other team's players to get the ball.
The ball tears through the goalie's gloves.

S'mores

by Megan Berry

Sitting by the campfire,
Crackle goes the logs.
Sun disappearing in the distance,
Fireflies are coming out.
My thoughts begin to wander,
My belly starts to rumble.
Marshmallow, chocolate, and graham crackers
Marshmallow on a stick
Roasted golden brown.
Chocolate placed on top of the graham cracker
Waiting for its gooey friend.
Squeeze them all together
Marshmallow oozing out,
Raise it up to my waiting mouth.
Marshmallow, chocolate, and graham crackers
S'mores hit the spot!

Spring Break

by Megan Berry

Started my trip on a plane,
Nine and a half hours, insane!

"Fall asleep," my parents demanded.
Munich, Germany is where we landed.

Toured the city on bike
What's not to like?

Second leg of the trip –
Florence, Italy in a zip.

Climbed hundreds of flights
To take pictures from great heights.

Our final stop was in Rome,
Then a long plane trip to go home.

Lego Ships

by Brendan Bjork

I like to build ships
Ships with Legos
I like to build ocean liners and warships
Ships with power functions
I like large warships with big guns
I like mid-size ocean liners
I build shipyards to build my ships
I build piers—five of them—for my ships
I like to build my ships to go in water
I named my company the Yellow Star Line
I build my warships to be heavy and large
I like them to be streamlined
I like to make warships to last for two months
I sometimes build ocean liners 36 inches or longer
I sometimes redo the whole superstructure
I build my ships in less than three hours
I love my ships from stem to stern.

Summer

by Brendan Bjork

Sunny summer is almost here
But the bluest blue lake is still cold and clear.
Winter jackets, stuff stored, things of the past,
Summer, like lightning, is coming; it's coming fast.

Hot summer is for fooling around and relaxing.
Summer, even with AC, is not for homework and faxing.
Heavy hard work is almost doubly done,
Summer brings fun under the bright yellow sun.

Swimming in the water cooling cool,
Jumping jacks in the swimming pool.
Sports bring out lots of fanatic fans,
Fourth of July has musical, military, marching bands.

Best Friends

by Mary Bolog

Best friends you keep forever
They accept you for who you are
They understand you
And you understand them.
You both know each other better
Than you know yourselves.
They're always there for you
Even when the situation is stupid
You act like you really care.
You argue about the silliest things,
Then get bored of fighting
And agree on something.
When you laugh, you laugh
Even if it is for no reason at all.
But the most important thing
To remember that makes
A best friend a best friend is:
No matter how much you annoy each other
You love each other more than the world.

Four Haikus

by Mary Bolog

The countdown begins.
They shout five, four, three, two, one.
Boom! Detonation.

When the wind blows hard,
The horrible hurricane's
Deadly waters rise.

What a thunderstorm!
Burning flashes of bright light.
Rain hitting window.

Mismatching my socks.
Who wears matched pairs anyway?
They won't see my socks.

Fear

by Grace Borchardt

I have a secret
Does it too?
The quiet thing I thought knew
Continually makes me frightened.
I have to wonder
Does it see me
Or am I out of sight
Hidden in the shadows?
It creeps at me
Slowly waiting to attack
Sleeping in my bed at night.
I hear it coming closer.
It chases me around my house
Until it gets what it wants:
Fear, fear, and more fear;
It hungers for all fear.

Three Haikus

by Grace Borchardt

Haikus are easy
But sometimes they don't make sense.
I like to eat fruit.

I'm a bad poet
Poetry is hard for me.
Like this line right here.

I like to eat food
Especially all junk food
You can eat the rest.

Ice Skating

by Arianna Bosco

Going to the rink
Almost late for my lesson.
My coach was waiting
But I still have to warm up.
What am I going to do?
Rushing out of my car
Running as fast as a racecar.
The door doesn't open,
Then it does.

Getting my skates on
My hands hurt so bad,
My laces are so sharp.
It's 3:29,
I've only got one minute,
Still have to tie one skate.
Now it's 3:30,
My coach is probably mad.
Now have work to do,
Have to skate for one hour.
No way, I can't do that,
I've got better things to do.

Then she said it was fine,
And I was very happy.
She said, "I was just kidding,"
And said my lesson was at 3:45.
So my Mom lied,
I rushed all my time
I could have warmed up,
Then acted all lazy
And waited unit my lesson started.

Starbucks Trip

by Arianna Bosco

I love Starbucks so much
I almost had it for lunch.
It was so yummy
It melted in my tummy.
I had a frappuccino
Then went to my friend Gino.
He asked for a sip
Only for a tip!
Gave me a dollar
As much as my dog's collar.
He took a sip
And bit his lip.
I went away
For a day.
He thought I was coming back
Because I didn't pack.
I came back with a tea
We both went to the sea.
We went to catch some fish
Then made a delicious dish.

Wolf

by James Castro

Wolves are grey.
They will never be by the bay,
Fluffy coat, eyes blazing fire, hardly gentle,
And are elemental,
But may be nice.
Just don't get too close, or you'll have to pay the price.
They love the cold
And can stand it because they are bold.
Wolves are fearless
And also tearless.
They're actually a type of dog
Nothing like a tree frog.
Have pointy teeth
And their jaws are as big as a wreath.
Wolves are the princes of snow
And will make you into their dough.
They eat anything with red blood
And will make it flood.
Other than that wolves are great,
Just don't act like the bait.

Angels

by James Castro

They watch over you,
They never say "Boo!"
Angels will always protect you protect you,
It is true, I'm not lying.
They have wings,
Not the barbeque kind!
And also are by your side
And will never hide.
The most famous is St. Michael.
Angels will guide you
And will never not.
If you need extra angel patrols, then say "Guardian angel."
Why do many people have fears?
They have someone right by their side.
So, no more tears!
Just don't wait for them to appear.

Friendship

by Kara Clark

Friendship is a rainbow at the end of a rainstorm.
Friendship is a cool breeze on a warm summer day.
Friendship is a warm fuzzy puppy lying across my lap.
Friendship is dancing to the beat.
Friendship is people wanting to spend time together,
To share laughter and tears, in good times and bad.
Friendship is people wanting to support one another.
Friendship is knowing there will always be someone to talk to.
I know they will be there for me.
I know that I will be there for them.
Friendship is someone to have sleepovers with.
Friendship is having the best day of your life.
Friendship is never-ending conversations.
Friendship is swimming on a hot summer day.
Friendship is someone there for a lifetime.
Friendship is something I share.

Four Haikus

by Kara Clark

Future is ahead.
Time flies so fast to rush past.
Never looking back.

I squint at the screen
I Snapchat and Instagram
I text all day long.

Colors after rain
Red, orange, yellow, green, blue.
Don't forget purple.

Gardens grow in spring.
Roses and lilies stand tall.
Spring, spring, hurry fast!

Day with Dad

by Trey Connolly

He gets home from work
Earlier than usual,
Tells me to get in the car.
We drive for a while
Look out the window, see the court.
Get out of the car and put on our shoes.
Play for a while, get back in the hot car,
Drive again, to the diner.
Go in and order,
When they bring out the hamburgers, you can see the steam.
Have dessert,
A piece of chocolate cake.
Head home, we talk and we laugh.
Such a good day,
But all good things must come to an end,
Just like a day with Dad.

Poem

by Trey Connolly

I am not here to tell you about my day,
That is not at all what I am going to say.
I am not ready
That is why this is a little unsteady.
I am not trying to waste your time
Just trying to rhyme.
This is too hard!
I would rather play with a card
Or eat candy,
It makes me feel dandy.
I don't want to be doing this
Rather be playing with my sis!
This poem is coming to an end,
I will have to say, "Goodbye, my friend."
There is no more time to talk,
So, I might go on a walk.
I have nothing else to say,
So, I hope you have a good day.
Now I have to leave
There is no need to grieve.

Sherlock Holmes

by Claudia Copher

Sherlock Holmes
Has fallen,
But he's not gone.
He's hiding in the shadows,
Lying low behind walls.
He'll return another day,
He won't be gone long.
I'll wait for him.
After all, we're a match,
Friendships should last
Even in death
(Or so you think).
You can't blame him
For being an angel.
He'll return, after all,
He's Sherlock Holmes.

The Ood

by Claudia Copher

The Ood are gone
But they are not dead
They are singing a song
Right under your bed
But do not fear
For they are here
Taking a break,
And eating some bread
I think that it's
Kind of a dread
That they'd rather do
That instead
But that's okay
As long as they
Mow the lawn
And aren't up until dawn
Look at that one,
Over there,
Wait, why does it
Have a spear?

Ice Cream

by Elizabeth Curry

A few years ago
I was at a Brewers game.
We watched for a while, and
Then my uncle took me to get
Ice cream.
We made our way past
The other fans, watching the game
With extreme interest.
We climbed
The stairs up, and up, and up,
Until we reached the upper level.
When we reached the concession stand,
I got chocolate ice cream with whipped cream
And chocolate syrup in a dish.
It was cold as ice, and my
Tummy grumbled.
When I was done
My tummy was happy.

Say "Cheese!"

by Elizabeth Curry

Today is the day
Start your day with a smile
You'll be glad you did.

The world is so bright
Smile like a shiny star
The sun will grin back.

Smile with a friend
Smile with someone you meet
Just be nice and kind.

People smile back
All is good including you
Smile all day long.

Trust in your spirit
Be generous and smile
You will make fond friends.

Put on a smile
A smile is contagious
Show your pearly whites.

I give free smiles
You can make a difference
So smile all day.

Say "Cheese!" and make someone's day!

Frogs

by Katie Dabrowski

The frogs croaked all night long.
I sat listening.
"What were they saying?"
I wondered.
They are very noisy
For such small animals.
Their webbed feet and bulgy eyes,
On land and in water
Making noise all day and night.
Keeping the neighborhood awake
And alive,
Stopping once or twice if it rains.
Splish, splash, splosh!
Jumping in the water when I walk by
Then starting up again.
Gone in the winter,
And back in the summer.
Their croaking like a million tiny bells.

Wolves

by Katie Dabrowski

In the summer,
We're howling and running and hunting.
In the winter,
We're chasing and digging and playing.
Howling to the moon,
Calling to each other,
Eating and napping
Whenever we like.
Out fur soft like rabbit's feet,
Our teeth sharp like huntsman's spears,
Until we grow older
And have pups of our own.

Piano

by Alexandra Daher

My piano is very smart you see
My piano loves me.
My piano knows when I'm happy
Because I play songs that are quick and snappy.
My piano know when I'm sad
And lets me play until I'm glad.
My piano knows when I'm in grief,
It lets me play songs beyond belief.
When I am under stress
And am all in a mess
I go to my piano to take a break
And an hour later, a song I make.
My piano is my life
If you touch it I will get out a knife
I love my piano and it loves me
If it could talk it would surely agree.

Pineapples

by Alexandra Daher

Pineapples are the fruit of life.
You open them with a knife.
They are my most favorite fruit.
And they are awfully cute.
Some are small
And some are quite tall.
Pineapples are the nicest fruit of them all.
They can even grow in the fall.
When you're eating pineapples
There's no room for sadness
Because pineapples fill you with gladness.
The inside of this fruit is a hidden treasure
Leaves a taste too great to measure.
Their insides are so sweet:
Bright yellow, juicy, and fun to eat.
It is a very tropical fruit.
It is special. It even wears a prickly suit.
Pineapples are my yellow fellow.
They are even better than jello!
Pineapples are so good and yummy
They satisfy everyone's tummy!

The Chicago Cubs

by Matthew Deacon

The Cubs are the best,
They will beat the rest.
The crack of the bat,
They all wear a baseball hat.

There is no contest,
They never take a rest.
The Cubs are at bat,
The other team scat.

You will be impressed,
Because they are the best.
They have never sat
Because they are always at bat.

Summer

by Matthew Deacon

Summer is fun.
There is no school,
There is no homework,
It is the best.

In the summer
You can do many things.
Such as
Swimming, sports, and much more.

You can stay outside
All day long,
Hang out with friends
And family.

Summer is awesome!
I like summer
I hope you do too!
SUMMER!!!!

Bears

by Emily Diab

Bears like to eat honey.
They sleep all winter.
They love fish.
There are black bears and brown bears,
They are majestic symbols of the wild.
As they roll in the leaves, it's hard to leave.
They have long claws.
Sometimes they're scary,
Sometimes they're sweet.
They have furry coats of fur.
They eat a lot.
They may seem cute,
But they can be violent.
They like to sleep.
They are lazy.

Willy Wonka

by Emily Diab

There is so much candy,
But there is no man named Mandy.
There is no man greater than Willy,
But he does not make chili!
Veruca might want a pink candy boat,
But the rest do not like her vote.
Violet likes to chew it,
But she does not listen a bit.
Mike is now small as a pea,
But can talk back as a buzzing bee.
Augustus loves to eat,
Especially meat!!!!!

Woodman's

by Tim Evans

Woodman's is a grocery store.
They sell many things
Such as dog treats and milk.
The produce is always ripe,
The meat is fresh.
We always get soy milk
Because my brother can't have dairy.
Let's finish the list:
Apples, oranges, bananas, and pears.
Sausage, bacon, ham, and cheese.
Man, do we have a feast.
Don't forget the milk and the ice cream.
Time to check out.
We put the items on the belt.
The price is $100.72.
We grab the receipt and leave.

Tiger

by Tim Evans

Tigers are cool.
They have razor sharp claws,
Skin patterns of orange and black,
Some swim in a pool.
They have humongous jaws.
Don't stare back.
They can be cruel.

Friendship

by Jalen Fayne

Friendship is the best,
They never give me a rest.
You can do fun stuff,
But I can't get enough!

My friends and I play football.
One of my friends is tall.
When we have sugar, we bounce off the wall!
They help you up when you fall,

Our friendship will never sail away.
They're always there when you wanna play.
It's good to have a friend who's always there,
And I'm glad they know I care.

I Love to Eat

by Jalen Fayne

I love to eat.
I eat a lot of junk food.
When I eat it, I get a rush.
I bounce off the wall.
My favorite junk food is Skittles,
I like to taste the rainbow.
I eat Louisiana hot sauce on my Doritos.
When I get home, I go to my room and eat.
You would find me in a coma from sugar;
Sometimes I get sick.
Chips, nachos, gum,
Juice, soda, Starburst,
Chocolate, cookies,
Fruit snacks,
Brownies, cupcakes.
I love to eat.

Music

by Reyna Ferraro

Music can be fun to listen to
But also sad;
There are lots of singers
In the music business.
You can jam out to
A lot of different songs
By a ton of talented
Artists,
Like Beyonce and Jay Z.
Boy bands are good, too.
It's cool listening to older
Songs by older artists.
My friends listen to
A big variety of music;
It's fun to see what kind
Of music they like.
Music is passion for some people,
Like my friends and me.

Shopping

by Reyna Ferraro

Shopping is a passion
For people with some fashion.
Don't expect anything less,
When she has the dress!
You fall in love with the heels
That are a great deal.
Even though you like what you see, you need to keep a ration
It causes a lot of frustration.
To have the best express dress
Comes with a lot of stress!
This new necklace that is teal
Will look good with my steering wheel!

Nature

by Ben Franklin

There once was a forest that stands tall,
But from a distance it seems real small.
For the grass has bright skin,
So that it stands with the rest of its kin.
And the animals are gentle
For they look for a place to settle
Although no humans have ever been here.
One little boy followed a deer.
The boy was nice as an angel
And as curious as a beagle.
Now and then
He would come play with the animals.

Crush

by Ben Franklin

There was a 16-year-old boy
Who had a crush on a girl.
He asked what was her name.
She said, "Ashley."
Time passed,
They became friends.
One day
He asked her on a date.
She said, "Yes."
On their fifteenth date
They kissed.
When he got home
He got excited,
So he decided to write a poem.
It was about them when they first met.
The next day
He got to school
And saw her.
He gave it to her.
She was flattered.
Then he asked her
If she would like to come to his house.
She said, "I would but..."
She said she had piano lessons,
So she suggested another day.
A couple days later
He found out that she was out of town.
He was sad,
Hoping to see her again.

Searching for My Dreams

by Katherine Gapinski

Even as I've known my past
I still act so scared like I don't know a thing.
Now, my past is the present.
You give strength to the darkness in the world.
My heart seems to be looking at a dream.
A promise that cannot be replaced
Is now within you
Jumping high from my dreams
No matter what happens, I'll be there.
Even though I am weak,
I can do whatever, as long as you're with me.
Until that one day I will be screaming your name.
Along the city streets
The moon will be glowing
With you right beside me.

A Friend

by Katherine Gapinski

The blue and black glasses that hide the significant blue-green
 eyes.
A smile as warming as the summer sun.
Her brown-blonde highlighted hair like a coconut.
The sarcastic voice that makes your face a little mad,
But there's always the sweet voice that covers it all.
Her annoying voice, along with the others.
Candy makes her hyper, and when you make her mad she
 gets aggressive, and argues.
She makes up syndromes, and can be inappropriate at times,
 but always comes through with her weird dancing.
She tried to help people doing a "mission", almost failed, but
 kept trying through it all.
She has made memories from stepping on a basketball court
 and getting fouled out, to fighting over a mic at a
 Christmas concert.
The people who leave their Christmas lights up, the horrible
 Mia Dynasty,
Orangey smell on hands, moving when needed to,
And waking up during naps by other people
Make her as angry as a fat person who drops their ice-cream.
Music, faces, insults, crabs, cat crabs, pickles, bunnies,
 sarcasm, meat, beef, sweets, and video games make
 her as happy as girls at Starbucks.
I love her, but she's sassy, and smart, pretty, and helps
 everyone in her path.
Long live the Katherine Dynasty, and cat crabs.

Eagles

by Jake Gessert

Eagles are cool
Flying high in the sky
They make nests
And attack people
They protect their eggs
They have big claws
And a big beak
They are the symbol of America
They eat fish
Fly from tree to tree
They are cool
They are my favorite bird
I love them
Like my family
Eagles, Eagles, Eagles
Are awesome!

Squirrels

by Jake Gessert

Squirrels jump,
Squirrels run.
They also collect nuts.
They can fly in the sky.
Oh, how I love squirrels!
Sometimes they're nice,
Sometimes they're mean.
They also like peanut butter,
But hate us humans.
They like to climb trees
And power lines.
They are fast,
But I love the fat ones.
Oh, how I love squirrels!
They eat bugs,
Sleep in nests
Really high up,
But they ruin your yards.
That is what is so bad about them.
Oh, squirrels!

Nature

by Jena Gessert

Nature is beautiful
It's always right there
It is cold, cool, warm, and hot.
Flowers growing
Birds singing
Kids playing
Dogs running
Animals in the shade
Wind is blowing
Swing swinging
Waves crashing
Sand in your toes
Stars shining
Fire is burning
Night time breeze
Nature is beautiful.

Summer Activity

by Jena Gessert

Summer's breeze
Allergies make you sneeze
You float in the pool
Oh, summer's so cool!

Sand gets stuck in your toes
Wash them off with a hose
I love ocean waves
I swim in a cave.

I bounce so high
I can touch the sky
I do a flip
I am very quick.

Baseball Night

by Dominik Gillespie

The night air was cool
The lights were bright
One hour after school
Our team was feeling right.

Our team fell behind
But we played tough
Our defense was kind
Our luck proved rough.

Our coach kept up our cheer
And we fought back
We still had no fear
Our bats began the attack.

Two runners were on base
And Hayden at the plate
A home run was the case
That changed our fate.

We tied the game
And our spirit was high
Our team had no shame
No one was shy!

Sports

by Dominik Gillespie

There is nothing better than getting tan and getting Vitamin D
    in your blood
You can play under the lights and in the rain
There is nothing better than to play on that rough turf
You can slam the basketball like Michael Jordan
Prove yourself like Jackie Robinson
Save hockey pucks like Corey Crawford
Have soccer moves like Cristiano Ronaldo
Run like Usain Bolt
Hit a home run like Albert Pujols
Intercept touchdown passes like Richard Sherman
There is nothing better than to make the game-winning save
Sports is in PE with gyms as hot as saunas
People might be boasters and snots
There is nothing more to say
Dream big and play hard.

Cupcake

by Lara Gonzalez

They put me in the oven to bake.
Me, a deprived and miserable cake.
Feeling the heat, I started to bubble.
Watching the others, I knew I was in trouble.

They opened the door and I started my life.
Frosting me with a silver knife.
Decorating me with candy jewels.
The rest of my batch looked like fools.

Lifting me up, she took off my wrapper.
Feeling the breeze, I wanted to slap her.
Opening her mouth with shiny teeth inside.
This was the day this cupcake had died.

The Flower

by Lara Gonzalez

There is a pot
With four yellow flowers
And many leaves.

The flowers have thick stems.
They are also green.
Their leaves have weird shapes
Almost like hands.

The flowers are curved.
They have an orange center.
They look like tacos.

They curl around
Then lean over to the side,
Longer on one side.

There are many stems,
But only four flowers.
How can that be?

Soccer

by Katie Hamm

Dribble, pass, shoot, score.
What's better than that?
All the fans cheering,
You know you have support.
Whether you win or lose,
Try your hardest, and
Remember you can always improve.
Practice in the sun,
You'll for sure get hot.
Dedicate time and you'll get there.
Work hard and play hard.
Talent only gets you so far,
You have to go the rest of the way.
You don't have to be good to practice,
You have to practice to be good.
So go, try soccer once.

Three Haikus

by Katie Hamm

What has blizzards and
Lots of snow? Winter, that's right!
It's like an ice cube!

No school, all play. At
The beach and many parks. I
Love summer so much.

Groundhog? Is it spring?
Take winter away. Let the
Flowers start to bloom.

Sweets!

by Stella Harrington

Chocolate is my favorite sweet of all!
It is soft and creamy,
And completely dreamy.
UMMM!! I also like gum! G-U-M!! GUM!!
Gum chewing is fine when it is once in a while, it
Stops you from smoking and it brightens your smile!
Another one of my favorite sweets is suckers!!
AKA lollipops! Lollipops give me energy to go to
Shop and buy a lot of stuff.
TWIX! TWIX! TWIX! Yummy ole Twix!!
Twix help me have huge and great big kicks for soccer!!
Which reminds me . . . Reese's!!
Reese's also help make even a better candy! —
Reese's Pieces!!!!
I love all candy but it is too hard to name them all,
Otherwise, I would!!
I could keep reading the list forever and ever and ever!
But that would take too long,
So here are some of my favorites!!!

The Bearded Man

by Stella Harrington

There once was a man with a beard,
Who everybody hated and feared,
The man was so sad,
Until he met his friend Chad,
And he became so happy he cheered,
But everyone still thought he was weird.
He was super glad,
That he finally had a friend named Chad,
But all the kids still hated him and sneered.
Finally, he cleaned his beard and it was cleared,
But he still was mad,
So he made a new friend named Brad.

The Seasons

by Eliana Hudock

Winter has some wonderful pictures.
In winter there are soft snowflakes,
There are also some very cool sculptures.
You will always find something new when you awake.

In spring, there are new things to discover.
There is lots of sunshine,
The world is beginning to have color,
And new things are beginning to grow just fine!

The hottest season is summer.
The days are longer and school is done.
The days are filled with wonder
This is the time to have much fun!

Autumn is very colorful, so don't be vain,
Autumn is full of a lot of change.
There is a lot of wind and rain,
Autumn is not very strange.

Animals

by Eliana Hudock

Animals are cool. One animal is a frog.
They're amphibians
That have very sticky tongues.
Some of them are poisonous.

Penguins live up south
Like a polar bear does.
Penguins eat much fish.
They are birds that do not fly
Like ostrich and flamingo.

Monkeys are funny.
They are also really smart,
And dolphins are, too.
Monkeys are very curious,
And their favorite food is fruit.

Birds are really cool.
There are many different kinds.
Birds love to fly free.
They are small spots in the sky,
And are nature's alarm clock.

Bird

by Valentin Iaquinta

Riding the wind like a water skier cruises over his wake.
Its feather-covered skis glisten beautifully in the summer sun.

Gliding like a runner down a winding road;
Clad with a feathery singlet that shines a metallic blue against
	the fluffy white track.

Its body seems lighter than air;
Floating like a freshly blown bubble in the breeze.

It is a great king,
Crowned with a headdress woven by God.

It is one star in an overflowing night sky,
Yet it stands out like a like a large oak tree in the middle of a
	field.

It is a warrior;
Willing to give its life to protect its family.

It is a lighthouse on a foggy evening;
Guiding its young into adulthood.

Its claws are two tiny spiders.
Small but extremely powerful.

Flight

by Valentin Iaquinta

I used to pilot an F-22.
Over the enemy I flew.
I traveled the speed of sound,
Propelled by flames burning bright blue.

When I flew in my F-16,
By Charlie I couldn't be seen.
I fell right out of the sky.
On that, I wasn't too keen.

I tried flying an F-35.
I'm lucky to still be alive.
If my opponents were a bunch of bees,
You could say I flew into their hive.

I once flew a P-6,
And yet, it wasn't that fun.
I managed to run out of fuel
Before my flight was done.

After I flew in my F-6,
It wasn't an easy fix.
Because right after my crash,
The plane's pieces were all in a mix.

The Wonderful Day

by Emma Iwen

The sun was shining like gold in the sky.
The wind was blowing a gentle breeze.
I hear the birds chirping a song that I can play.
The green lush grass was like a soft blanket.
The trees were creaking when they would sway.
The bushes were rustling away.
He looked inside and had nothing to say.
OH, LOOK! Baby bunnies, what a surprise!
He left them alone and lay back down.
My, what a wonderful day.
Oh, how the clouds were moving so smoothly.
It was like a bird flying through the sky.
Suddenly, a robin flew by.
I feel the warmth of the sun on my skin.
It makes me feel energized.
Friends are playing in their yards.
I hear the ice cream truck in the distance.
What kind shall I have?
Could today be any better?
What a wonderful day!

Baby Animals

by Emma Iwen

Baby animals are small and cute.
Baby alligators are tiny, but bite hard.
Baby birds, chirping for food.
The baby seal is swimming.
Alligators, birds, and seals, oh my.

Baby lions roar like kittens.
Baby ducks are trying to fly.
Baby snakes are slithering around.
Now my mom is on the hunt.
Lions, ducks, and snakes, oh my.

Baby frogs giving their tails away.
The baby foal trying to stand on wobbly legs.
Baby bunnies are trying to hop.
Frogs, foal, and bunnies, oh my.
Baby animals are so cute and cuddly.

Cookies

by Emma Johnson

The dough is baking at 350 degrees,
While they are cooking all I can hear is pleas.
Can I please have one?
When will they be done?
My mom said the cookies will be done faster than you think.
In fact, done before you can blink!
They sit perfectly aligned on metal trays.
In five minutes all the dough will raise.
Those five minutes went by very fast.
The cookies now look very vast.
The oven begins to make a beeping noise,
In come all the hungry boys.
My mom takes out the metal rack,
The cookies looked good, that's a fact!
The cookies were eaten, one by one.
Yes! The cookies are finally done.

Positive

by Emma Johnson

There once was a little girl,
Who was very short and happy.
She loved to spin and twirl,
After that she got very nappy.
She was never mad,
And did not like to frown.
If she saw someone un-glad,
She would turn that frown upside-down.
She spread so many good vibrations,
And she had so many friends,
Her life was a celebration
Of good things that will never end.

Cereal: A Poem in Seven Haikus

by Keely Kennedy

Cereal is good
Cheerios, Chex, Mini Wheats
Fruity and frosted

Cinnamon Toast Crunch
Fiber One and Honey Comb
Crunch Berries and Trix

Reese's Puffs and Pops
Apple Jacks and Frosted Flakes
Raisin Bran and Kix

Lucky Charms and Oh's
General Mills and Kellogg's
Fruit Loops and Total

Crispy and crunchy
Sometimes gets stuck between teeth
Nuggets and circles

Flakes and chocolate
Flowers and stars and cool swirls
Very colorful

I love to eat it
I love all of the flavors
Cereal is good.

Hunting

by Keely Kennedy

Hunting is fun,
But you have to wait a long time
To see a deer.
You have to be warm
And wear lots of layers.
Silence is mandatory while hunting.

Once you see a deer,
You look through the scope
And find the spot
Between the shoulder
And the front leg.
You pull the trigger.
You wait for it to drop
And then run to find it.

You take out the guts.
You drag the deer
Out of the woods.
You might need help,
Unless you tie the legs to
A sturdy stick and carry it out,
Indian-style.

You've shot your first deer.
Be very proud of yourself.
Skin the deer and
Dry out the fur.
You can share the meat,
Or not.

You've been hunting
And was it fun?
Of course it was.

Country Life

by Matthew Knapp

Calming,
Togetherness,
Family,
Helping,
A way of life.

Grass growing,
Trees blooming,
Wheat sprouting,
Flowers blooming,
Corn sprouting.

Crocuses,
Tulips,
Daffodils,
Bright colors,
Fresh flowers.

Birds chirping,
Bees buzzing,
Frogs croaking,
Lambs baaing,
Lightning bugs blinking.

Helping hands,
Working together,
Sharing talents,
Family picnics,
Laughing at family stories.

This is a way of life
That brings joy.
Close friends and family
Together
As a daily way of life.

Hunting

by Matthew Knapp

The season is fall.
The leaves are turning orange, yellow, red.
The birds are getting ready to hide,
Knowing the people in orange are soon to be arriving.

The smell of fall is in the air,
The grass is turning brown.
The dogs are getting ready to run,
To sniff out the bird that is hiding in the grass.

Oh, no! I hear the dogs coming!
What am I to do?
I have lost track of how much time I had,
I cannot run, 'cause here they come!

I sit tight in the waving grass,
The steps are getting louder and louder.
They see me hiding and "BANG!" I hear.
The dog has turned and safety is near.

My Mother

by Josephine Knight

I love my mother!
She is so sweet.
She is helpful.
She is very smart.
She loves me.
She cares for me.
She makes delicious food.
She bakes yummy muffins.
She is my chauffeur.
She comforts me.
She cheers me on when I am winning or losing.
She puts a smile on my face when I need a laugh.
She cares for me when I'm sick.
She encourages me to do my best.
She plays games with me.
I love my mom!

Monsters

by Josephine Knight

I don't like monsters.
They hide in my closet and under my bed.
They look like lobsters.
They love to eat my bread.
They are fuzzy, scary, thingamajigs.

Five Seconds of Summer

by Katie Kormylo

There's this band,
I want them in my hand.
They aren't that famous.
Don't blame us,
We love them so much!
Their music has a soft touch.
They are my cup of tea,
Not my peas,
Ewww!
There are only a few,
Actually four,
But I want more!

Fruit

by Katie Kormylo

Fruit is good,
So is cheese.
I like them all.
Some fruits are very tall,
Some are small.
Pineapples, apples, of all shapes and sizes.
No.
You're making me drool!
I love all fruit,
It's very cute.
Cheese, please.
Gouda, brie, and mozzarella –
Very bella.
That's Italian for beautiful
Not pitiful.

Sorry, Gotta Run!

by Katherine Lesavich

I would love to stay and chat,
But I've really gotta run.
Sorry to disappoint you,
But we'll talk when I am done.

No way to get out of it,
It's just something that I do.
I'll just run a few miles,
When I'm done, I'll talk to you.

Ok, I'm finally finished,
Now what did you want to say?
Hold on, it's hard to hear you,
I'll run over, on my way!

Love

by Katherine Lesavich

Love can be many different things, feelings or emotions!
Love can be happy,
Love can be sad,
Love can be confusing.
But it's all worth it once you've found your true love.
Love is one of the best feelings in the world,
It can also be one of the worst.
Everybody wants love,
Everybody wants to find their Mr. or Ms. Right.
But how do you know when you've found love?
How do you know when a person is your soul mate?
Sometimes, you don't know.
Sometimes, only time knows.
You have to wait...and...wait.
Other times, true love finds you.
Love is as complicated as a huge maze.
It has twists and turns.
There's times when you think you know the way out,
But it's just another wall of problems, jealousy, anger, and drama.
In the maze of love, there are often two paths,
One of them leads to heartbreak,
The other leads to the ending,
The way out,
Your soul mate.

My Dog

by Matthew Lesperance

My dog is nice.
My dog likes ice.
My dog is good.
My dog eats wood.

My dog is brown.
My dog has claws.
My dog is cute.
My dog eats wood.

My dog is nice.
My dog is good.
My dog likes ice.
My dog eats wood.

Young Love

by Leah Madden

The teenage boy so young and so flustered
Sat in wonder about the girl he loved.
Her long gorgeous hair that flew in the wind,
Her teeth that were as white as a blank piece of paper.
Her eyes so big and so brown,
He sat and wondered
Did she like him too?
But why would she like him?
He started to stare,
He wanted to talk,
But his voice was not there.
If he had one more day he would tell her he loved her.

His big blue-green eyes,
So large and so round
Looked up at the shy girl.
Her big brown eyes looked up at him.
He smiled so wide and so big.
She smiled back with a wink.

Two Haikus

by Leah Madden

Presents under tree.
Santa Claus eating cookies.
Christmas time is here.

Summer is coming.
Swimming in the burning sun.
Summer is my favorite.

Hamburgers

by Anthony Madrigrano

Hamburgers, I eat, all day long
Delicious with every bite I take.
Sometimes I like ketchup and pickles,
Usually onions on the top.
I always get them from McDonald's.
Only one dollar, even I can pay.
I usually get French fries on the side or on my burger.
Never, ever, give me tomatoes on my burger.
If you do, you better beware!
But if you get it right, you get a tip.

Lobster

by Anthony Madrigrano

Lobster I love, will never hate.
Eat all the time, even with a steak.
Always from Red Lobster,
Sometimes from Joe's Crab Shack,
Never from anywhere else.
Melted butter on the side,
Never on the top.
Crack the claws open to eat,
Dip it in the butter,
I eat it, wipe dripping butter from my cheek,
Delicious!

Rosie

by Solei Maj

Violets are blue.
My Rose is black.
Her eyes are black as coal.

Long ears are a flowing black river streaming
Down her shoulders.
"Yip-yip," she says hello.

In the morning, I wake up to a nose as wet as a hose in my face,
And at the corner of my eye I see a tail, tiny as a cheese curd, wagging.
Her breath is as heavy as elephants when
They're walking through a hot jungle that has no water.

Seasons

by Solei Maj

Snow is white and fun.
It sparkles brightly in the sun,
It falls from the sky.

Spring is cold and warm.
It is windy all day long,
The birds are chirping.

Summer is warm.
It gets a little cold out,
You can stay up late.

Leaves are changing fast.
In fall, you get to jump in them.
Most leaves are yellow.

Soccer

by Ellie Mandli

It takes time, skill, and practice,
Waking up before sunrise, and working till sundown.
You need to work your hardest,
To overcome struggles and become great.
Injuries are part of the game
You have to be better than the ones who came before,
And ones who will follow.
You need dedication and passion,
For the sport, your team, and coaches.
To build your skills and become great
Takes long hours, sweat, and tears.
Coaches teach you never to give up,
Not even when you're playing in the elements.
You will learn to play in all conditions,
Rain, snow, and blistering heat,
But you know you have to do it again tomorrow.

Lemonade

by Ellie Mandli

A lazy day upon the bay.
Nothing to do, nothing to say,
No places to be, no things to see,
No thoughts to chew,
No bills for me.
Cool lemonade in my throat
Complements my rocking boat,
And I find myself drifting away,
Away.
I find myself drifting away.
Passing by islands, ships, other things of that sort.
I sail into the sun, on such a mild day,
Not a thought to chew,
Not a bill to pay.
Lemonade.

The Tippity-Tap-Tap Bubble Wrap

by Mia Marotti

Tippity-tap-tap,
Goes the bubble wrap.
Grace smiles at me.
I touch the plastic top,
Which is as soft as a mop,
I press one hand and feel free.

Tippity-tap-tap
Goes the bubble wrap,
Others pop as well with glee.
BANG! Another circle goes pop,
Claudia tells us to stop,
Exploded sheets flee.

Tippity-tap-tap
Goes the bubble wrap,
My ears begin to dree.
Classmates warn us to make the noise drop,
But then...
Ms. Davidson shouts that we have to be done,
Which means to stop our fun,
And marks the end of the tippity-tap-tap bubble wrap.

I Hate Pumpkin Pie

by Mia Marotti

I hate pumpkin pie,
It sure makes me want to die.
I want to throw it in the trash,
It's not worth any cash!
I say I love it but that's a lie,
When I eat it, my mouth is dry.
The gooey center makes me dash,
When I see it, I'm gone in a flash!
I hate all parts of pumpkin pie,
Even the whipped cream makes me cry!
The crust is like flavorless ash,
If it was a person, it would be brash!
Oh how I hate pumpkin pie.

Push

by Claire Mayew Sherman

Ever since I was four, I've been told
The world was mine.
I could do what I wanted to do.
I didn't realize I found what I wanted to at the age of eight.
I didn't realize I found my passion.
I started to practice, put time in.
Work, work, mess up, work, work, mess up.
I know this life isn't easy.
I know it's really hard to make a living out of this,
As everyone keeps reminding me.
I know it's one in a million.
Why can't I be the one?
Don't tell me I can't do it.
No one has ever seen how much time I've put in.
Don't say practice won't help.
Sure it will.
Though I may not be big enough, strong enough,
Fast enough or even good enough right now...
I know I have pushed myself.
I am proud.
Don't tell me I can't do it.
No one knows my passion and drive.
And in the process of becoming the best I can be
I'm following my dreams.
Those dreams may or may not come true...
But it won't be because I didn't push myself.

Life

by Claire Mayew Sherman

Life is too short for sitting around.
Too short to be wasting time arguing with each other.
Too short to be afraid to be yourself.
Too short to not follow your dreams.
Why do we insist on making everything complicated?
Life isn't easy,
But it's not impossible.
Why are people wasting their time procrastinating?
Instead of doing what they are supposed to.
Before we know it, BOOM!
Our lives are half over.
And we spent our time doing nothing,
Except feeling sorry for ourselves.
What happened to seizing the day?
I ask myself that every single day.

Flowers

by Abygale McGonigle

Soft and fragile petals
Drooping under the sun's rays
Opening their arms to the fresh air
And morning dew.

Colors splash across the yard,
Like Skittles dancing in front of my eyes,
Swaying with the breeze
In perfect rhythm with nature

Standing tall like soldiers
Waiting for their orders
To open with the light
Or close with the darkness.

Slow march to death
As weather grows colder
Rain turns to snow
And white frost covers the ground.

Pigs

by Abygale McGonigle

I like pigs.
They like to dig.
They roll in the dirt.
They don't wear shirts.
Pigs hate bacon.
They don't want to be taken.
Pigs are super cool.
I draw pictures of them at school.
They are really fun.
I enjoy watching them run.
Pigs are my favorite creatures.
They have attractive features.

Mothers

by Marlena Moore

I took for granted when I was small,
That that was that, and that was all.
But now it dawns on me like in a dream,
That things are more than what they seem.
The roles we watch our mothers play,
Mean more to me each passing day.
I feel she's with me every stride.
It warms my heart and all inside.
Of course she teaches right and wrong,
And has been there for me all along,
And does the things that Mothers do,
But does it more than I ever knew.
Who would have ever guessed,
I'd be so sweetly blessed,
To have an angel all my own,
So I would never feel alone.
Moms were made with divine intents,
To work on Earth as secret agents.
She gives a glimpse of what Heaven could be,
And with a kiss, passes it along to me.

Spring Awakening

by Marlena Moore

Spring's eyes open from her slumber,
Sees pinks and greens, not ash and umber.
Birds return and chirp to greet her,
And bid farewell to Old Man Winter.

Refreshing the scene with her showers,
And bringing with it bursts of flowers.
When the short day's glum is flushed away,
She scents the air with floral spray.

Then she wraps herself in golden cloak,
Bringing warmth to all the folk.
Glistening light lengthens the day,
Giving us all more time to play.

Family Trip

by Natalie Murphy

Taking a drive through the woods, my heart full of glee,
It's just me and my parents, all on a trip are we.
Until the old family car came to a stop,
We were all out of gas, every single drop.
While we were sitting there trying to make the car go,
There was a rustling in the trees... a fawn and a doe.
That fawn and that doe approached me with a glow in their eyes,
And I knew in my heart they weren't there to say their goodbyes.
Instead there was a look of hunger on their faces,
So I went into the car and grabbed all the snack cases.
I fed them the apples, the carrots, and celery galore,
Until there was nothing but crumbs on the forest floor.
A while later mother called me to go.
So I carefully walked up to the fawn and the doe.
I said, "Goodbye," trying not to cry,
For I would miss them so...
That fawn and that doe.

The Mist

by Michael Pienkos

The mist settles within the air
Hovering above the grassy plain.
Shimmering, slowly moving on,
As if a tapestry blowing in the wind.
It clings to the ground wishing not to leave
Like a child holding close to its mother.
Cooling the surrounding air,
Chilling to the bone,
Blurring the view behind.
Like a piece of glass, yet scratched and discarded.
Reflecting the light from the rising sun,
Creating a blinding but beautiful scene.
But as the light breaks through,
The mist knows its time is gone.
Slowly disappearing to dew,
I know my time here is through.

A Bad Morning

by Michael Pienkos

This morning I woke on the wrong side of bed,
The alarm scared me and I fell on my head.
As I started to stand,
I knew the day would not be grand.
But I got to my feet,
And went down to eat.
But when I noticed the time,
I couldn't eat my lime.
So I grabbed my lunch,
And ran off in a hunch.
But I barely missed the bus,
And I knew the morning was just a big fuss.

Books

by Bernadette Pitt-Payne

Reading is my favorite thing to do,
Fiction, mystery, and fantasy, too.
I'd read all day from morning to night
As long as there was a little light.
Long books, short books, books of all kinds,
Coming back from the library with great new finds.
To me, every book is a treasure,
That's why reading is my pleasure.
I could read for hours on end.
Watch and you'll see, books are a new trend.
Reading books is fun to do.
Who knows? You may like it, too.

Roller Coasters

by Bernadette Pitt-Payne

You hear the raging rumble of the
Roller coaster
Before you have left the parking lot.
As soon as you're in the park
You run to the sign
Which puts you about fifth in line.
You are so close you can hear the coaster hiss
As it glides over the track.
As you get closer,
You smell the scent of food
Wafting from the nearby restaurant.
The day has grown as hot as a furnace
But you are almost on the ride.
The car stops.
You step in.
Fasten your seatbelt,
And as smooth as a pebble, it takes off.
After the ride,
You are all shook up inside.
You walk for a while
Then say, "Cool, we should do it again."

Friends

by Brendon Rafferty

Friends are the best,
They never give me rest.
Even if we fall,
We always have a ball.
Even if we fight,
We always have a good night.
Some friendships sail away,
But ours is here to stay.
Even if we almost die,
We're always flying high.
When we get in trouble,
We're there on the double.

Perseverance

by Brendon Rafferty

Never give up, always persevere.
Dedication beats medication,
There ain't no sky too high.
No sea too rough,
No guy too tough,
Pray for victory.
Even if you can see the finish line in sight,
Learn from your mistakes.
Dig for your last bit of endurance,
Turn all that criticism into energy.
Be a hard-bodied, hairy-chested, rootin', tootin' athlete or
       student.
Be yourself,
Push until you can't, and then some more.
And remember "F" is for "forget about it,"
And remember never to give up.

MLB

by Jake Reigel

A-Rod is overrated,
But don't make the same mistake, 'cause K-Rod is not related.
The best are McCutchen, Trout, and Cabrera,
Back then, it was Yogi Berra.
There are thirty teams in the Major League.
One is the Dodgers with their own Yasiel Puig.
Sure the Brewers are good,
And you'd expect that the D'backs should.
The Yankees have dollars signs,
While Wrigley Field has those vines.
The Astros are just sad,
They'll probably always be this bad.

Summer

by Jake Reigel

Summer is the best
But we are still very busy.
Between All-Star tournaments and basketball
I simply cannot find the time.
But I love summer regardless of what I do,
Whether I'm at the pool or doing yard work,
As long as I'm in summer I'm excited for the next day.
I have a summer goal to see every MLB stadium
And catch a game or two of the Kingfish.
I'm always happier in summer.
I don't mean to diss school, but I don't care about you.
In summer I don't need to be bright, as long as the sun does
      it for me. ·
I will have a little time outside of that stuff to mess with
      friends,
And when it's over I'll look back at what I did,
And regret what I didn't,
Then I will go back to the normal routine of school.

Pizza

by Tess Roberts

Pizza is my friend
I love it so much
On it I like cheese
Sometimes maybe with ham
It tastes good.

You put it in the oven
So you can eat it
It can come out
Crunchy or soft
But it still tastes good.

Many toppings
It doesn't matter
Which one you choose
Because they all taste good.
Which one will you choose?
It can be anything.

Sports

by Tess Roberts

Baseball, summertime fun
One, two, three strikes – "You're out!"
Line drives, fly balls, hit a home run,
Slide into home plate when you're in doubt.

Basketball is my favorite sport
Dribble, pass, and shoot to score,
Hustle up and down the court
Steal the ball and score some more.

Soccer is a game of feet,
Kick the ball to score a goal
At center field captains meet
Get set, go at the ref's roll.

Volleyball is what I like,
Serve the ball over the net,
Bump, set, spike,
We will win this game yet.

Football is a gridiron game,
It can cause a lot of pain
Lots of teams with funny names,
Football fans are just insane.

Music

by Seth Rosen

Music makes me want to dance.
It makes people happy when they're sad.
It entertains us in daily life,
And pulls us away from the stresses of daily life.
It's our gate from life itself.
It makes us think of different memories of family, friends, and
 just good times.
It doesn't matter who you are,
Music takes you very far –
From different countries
To imaginary places.
Music soothes the soul with ease,
And makes people feel free.
Music used in many ways –
From games to sleep,
Even toys.
When you're down and in a rut, music is your ticket up.

Two Friends

by Seth Rosen

I once had a friend named Jack,
He really liked to run track.
Although he never was as good as Val,
They were still good pals.
Until Jack broke his back.

My friend Joe really likes the snow,
Even though his dad says *no*.
Once he got very cold,
He froze and looked like he was a mold.
Should have listened to his dad's *no*.

My Mother

by Jonathan Rudd

My mother loves me like a bear with her cubs —
With her life.
She also is careful with a knife.
So everyday
My mom goes off to work.
She is a nurse, by the way.
Every day is pretty much normal,
But every other Friday we go with her.
And she drives six hours,
So she leaves early,
And usually with nobody but herself.
We stay in hotels
And live off of restaurants
And our suitcases.

Poor Old Jake

by Jonathan Rudd

Poor old Jake,
Got hit with a rake.
Right in his face,
It was a big disgrace
To his dad.
He thought he was bad.
Poor old Jake.

Haikus About My Life

by Caleb Ryherd

Kick the soccer ball.
The goalie misses the ball
We won the season.

I like my smart phone.
I can download games and apps.
I got it today.

I have a guitar.
It is a fun instrument.
I have an amp too.

I have a tablet.
I need to get a speaker
That is very loud.

I like my back pack.
It has a lot of pockets.
It can hold pencils.

I need medicine.
For some reason I need it.
I need it to heal.

Museum

by Caleb Ryherd

I went to the great museum.
The museum said to the art, "Get out of my stomach.
I keep getting more food in me."
The dinosaurs' bones said, "Get me some flesh.
I want to eat humans. I think they would be tasty.
There are so many people in here every day.
I can't move. I am afraid that I am stuck."
I wish I had something that can put me to sleep forever.
I want to get over into the dream world.

Worms

by Mia Scarlato

A worm's life is weird.
Their mouth looks like their butt.
They have no eyes.
They have no ears.
Then it rains,
And the worms flood out.
With children throwing them about.
Then returning to the ground
Where moles gobble them up.
Some may not return underground,
They dry up,
Get run over,
Get eaten,
And die.
A worm's life is hard.
Glad I'm not one.

Bella: Two Haikus

by Mia Scarlato

I watch you sleeping
And I buy you stuff sometimes.
I don't even mind.

I love you so much.
You are my number one friend.
My doggy, Bella.

Cookies

by Gabriella Schneider

Cookies come in many different shapes sizes and flavors.
Many cookies are made by professional bakers in white aprons and hats.
You can see the cookies through a glass display case.
Some are made by mothers at home in their kitchens.
Those cookies can be devoured on site!
Some cookies can be HUGE, others can be small.
Some cookies are circles, others can be made into different shapes.
Some are very elaborate, some are simple.
Cookies can be shaped like anything, from an Easter egg to a horse.
All cookies are fun to eat.

Lola

by Gabriella Schneider

Lola is my dog.
She eats like a hog!
She is very fluffy,
Her hair makes the air stuffy.
She likes to sleep at home,
But she also likes to roam.
She likes to run,
Though after isn't fun.
She has a little hobble,
Like a grandma with a wobble!
She likes to be pet,
And boy does she stink when wet!

Car Ride

by Emily Schwerdtfeger

We all get in the car and buckle up to start our trip.
Buckle up. Click.
Turn key. Car starts.
Turn on music. LOUD.
Start driving.
Destination unknown.
Roadway is rough.
Potholes laughing at us.
Cars speeding by like wild horses,
Untamed.
Street signs are shining rainbows of color.
Car making a clanking, clunking sound.
What could it be?
Suddenly we stop.
Car quits working.
Stranded on side of road.
Car ride all done.

Three Haikus

by Emily Schwerdtfeger

The Hobbit is cool.
It makes me really happy.
It is fun to watch.

My name is Pippin.
I am funny and foolish.
Merry is my friend.

I hold the one ring.
It is very powerful.
It makes me crazy.

Spring

by Matthew Spadafore

Spring has finally sprung.
Away our coats have been flung.
It is pretty warm
But once in a while there is a storm.
The birds will chirp.

We can do lots
Like plant pumpkins in our pots.
We cannot do ice hockey
But we can ride a Kawasaki!
Yay for spring!

There are lots of birds.
Some birds' names have many words.
Like the American Finch,
Or hummingbirds that are only an inch.
Many birds will sing.

But spring won't last forever,
So we have to make it the best spring ever!
I wish we could do them all,
But soon it will be summer, then fall.
So we should have fun — Spring has sprung!

The Stanley Cup

by Matthew Spadafore

Hockey is an intense game
To score more goals.
There are many positions:
Forward, defense, and goalie
And they all work hard
To get the thing they most desire.
In their dreams, they dream to win it.
In their lives, they play to win it.
But they must make great plays
Like amazing goals,
Or a shootout save.
And they must remember
That even if you lose,
You have to have fun.
But you should still try
To win the object of your dreams:
The silver Stanley Cup.

Love

by Ryan Spadafore

There is a girl that I adore.
That's all I'll say, and nothing more.
Her eyes shine with dazzling light.
The light they make is very bright.

She has a very bright warm smile.
That illuminates for about a mile.
Her gaze will always melt my heart.
She's sweeter than a raspberry tart.

This poem is true, yes it is.
The girl I like is the sweetest miss.
This, like all things must come to an end.
With her, my days I wish to spend.

Four Haikus

by Ryan Spadafore

What makes a good poem?
You have to choose your poem type.
This is a haiku.

Garbage disposal.
Makes a mutilating sound.
Crushes rotten things.

Seventy degrees.
Perfect weather for playing.
Stuck doing homework.

Kokopelli art:
Hunchback dude playing a flute,
With dancing legs, too.

In Summer

by Joseph Stapleton

In summer it is warm.
At times, it can storm.
It is a good time to stay outside.
Go for a swim or go exercise at the gym.
The best time is a long bike ride.

Go to the beach and play.
Or sit in the warm sun all day.
Move away from the sun and find a cool place to hide.
Build a fort in the sand using both hands.
But at the beach, beware of the tide.

Summer is a good time for a run.
When you go with your dog, you will have some fun.
In summer, people go to the lake.
It is a great time to go on a boat,
But remember it's windy, so bring your coat.
Summer is better than eating chocolate cake.

Rainy Day

by Joseph Stapleton

On a rainy day, there are many things to do inside.
You could play a board game or talk with friends.
You could also read in a quiet place.
You could draw your favorite dog.
You could play tug-of-war with your dog.
You could make a puzzle or play card games.
You could dig through old things and examine them.
If you get really bored, you could do homework.
You could play with Legos or have a Nerf battle with you
    brother.
You could also play hide-and-seek.
You could watch Sponge Bob Square Pants.
You could play video games.
You could excite your grandparents by talking on Skype.
You could stare out the window and watch the rain fall down.
If you get really bored, you could take a nap under a cozy
    blanket.
When rainy days come, there is a lot to do.

Dogs

by Ben VerHagen

Dogs are awesome animals.
They come in many sizes.
Some are big and some are small,
And all come with surprises.

They like to play around
With their strong teeth to bite.
They eat almost anything.
It gives me a little fright.

Most are big and strong,
But some are small and frail,
When they set out on a mission,
They almost never fail.

Often they like to act tough,
But under all the act,
They all have a huge soft spot,
I know this for a fact.

Pasta

by Ben VerHagen

I love food.
My favorite food is pasta.
I like it a lot.
It puts me in a good mood.
I love to eat it for lunch
With lots of sauce and meat.
If there was no pasta at all,
I'd rarely ever eat.
I like it for dinner as well.
I eat it as fast as a snake.
It's just that good and yummy
It always fills my tummy.
My dad is the best pasta-maker,
He puts meat and sauce and all that good stuff on it.
If I ate all the pasta
I doubt I would fit.
Pasta is the best food ever.
I bet the first pasta-maker was a genius.
Without pasta in my life
My life would be meaningless.

Copyright/Trademark Disclaimer

This book includes poems written by middle school students for a class writing project. These poems are protected by the legal doctrine of *Fair Use* as provided by 17 U.S.C. 107 of *U.S. copyright law* as they may include text related to commentary, criticism, parody, teaching and scholarship. Selected poems include trademarks of others. These trademarks are used under the legal doctrine of *Nominative Fair Use*, by which a person may use the trademark of another as a reference to describe a product or service. The trademarks used herein were used under the legal doctrine of Nominative Fair Use because: (1) the product or service could not be readily identified by the student without using the trademark; (2) the student only uses as much of the mark as is necessary for the identification; (3) the student has done nothing to suggest sponsorship or endorsement by the trademark holder; (4) the student has not used the mark in a disparaging manner; and (5) because the trademark use is only nominative fair use, it cannot and does not dilute the corresponding trademark in any way. However, if any trademark owner desires that their trademark be removed from this publication, please contact the publisher. The corresponding student poem including the trademark will be immediately removed from all new copies of this book.

St. Joseph Catholic Academy

St. Joseph Catholic Academy is a comprehensive Preschool through Senior High School, designed to educate the whole child. At all levels, 4K, Elementary, Middle and High School, SJCA upholds the highest ideals of scholarship, citizenship and faith.

At SJCA, each student is known, appreciated, loved and encouraged to be his or her very best self, academically, spiritually, socially and physically.

Our teachers know our students by name, and support them both in and out of the classroom. Likewise, they know our school families and work daily with them so that every student reaches his or her fullest potential.

Our sequential curriculum, high expectations, small learning environment and articulated Lancer Value System consistently yield independent, thoughtful scholars, creative, confident leaders and lifelong stewards.

www.kenoshastjoseph.com

ABOUT COCONUT AVENUE®, INC.

Coconut Avenue, Inc. is an award winning publishing company that publishes award winning books. Coconut Avenue was founded by *Stephen Lesavich, PhD, JD* (lesavich.com) in 2007, and is located in Chicago, Illinois. Dr. Lesavich, an award winning author, is considered by many to be a self-help pioneer and visionary.

Coconut Avenue was founded on South LaSalle Street in the financial district, the heartbeat and pulse of the city of Chicago.

Coconut Avenue publishes books in a variety of genres, in most popular print and electronic formats. Coconut Avenue books are available worldwide in bookstores and on major e-booksellers on the Internet.

Visit Coconut Avenue Online:
coconutavenue.com

COCONUT AVENUE®, INC.

Is proud to be the Publisher of the Award Winning Book:

*The Plastic Effect: How Urban Legends Influence
the Use and Misuse of Credit Cards*

Polly A. Bauer and Stephen Lesavich, PhD, JD

theplasticeffect.com

**2013 Independent Publisher Living Now
Book Award Winner**

**Recognizing the Year's Best Books for Better Living
Gold Medal Winner
Judged Best Book in the Finance/Budgeting Category**

"The Independent Publisher Living Now Book Awards celebrate the innovation and creativity of newly published books that enhance the quality of our lives and publicize the importance of these books to readers and their vitality in the marketplace."

If you are interested in discussing credit card topics, please join us on Twitter at the hash tag: **#THEPLASTICEFFECT**.

COCONUT AVENUE®, INC.

AWARD WINNING PUBLISHING COMPANY

Coconut Avenue, Inc. was selected for the **2014 Best of Chicago Award** in the *Publishing Consultants & Services* category by the Chicago Award Program.

"*The Chicago Award Program recognizes companies that enhance the positive image of small business through exceptional service to their customers and their community. These award winning companies help make the Chicago area a great place to live, work and play.*"

Coconut Avenue®
Chicago, Illinois USA

The Creative Avenue for Best Selling Authors®

Online: coconutavenue.com

Coconut Avenue, Inc. also publishes other books under the *Coconut Avenue Elite* imprint.

Coconut Avenue Elite
Online: ca-elite.com

OTHER COCONUT AVENUE® PRODUCTS

FOR MORE INFORMATION ABOUT OTHER COCONUT AVENUE® AUTHORS, BOOKS, PRODUCTS, AND EVENTS, PLEASE CONTACT:

Coconut Avenue, Inc.
39 S. LaSalle Street, Suite 325
Chicago, Illinois 60603 USA

(312) 419.9445 (v)
(312) 896.1539 (f)
email: info@coconutavenue.com
Online: coconutavenue.com

Coconut Avenue®

The Creative Avenue for Best Selling Authors®, Coconut Avenue®, The Creative Avenue For Best Selling Authors® and the Coconut Avenue graphic® are registered US Trademarks of Coconut Avenue, Inc.
Unauthorized use is prohibited.

If you are interested in discussing book publishing topics, please join us on Twitter at the hash tag **#COCONUTAVENUE**.

If you are interested in discussing poetry, please join us on Twitter at the hash tag: **#SIXSUGARSPOETRY**.

www.ingramcontent.com/pod-product-compliance
Lightning Source LLC
Chambersburg PA
CBHW051801040426
42446CB00007B/456